PAPER MOVIE MACHINES

by BUDD WENTZ

TROUBADOR PRESS, INC., SAN FRANCISCO
a subsidiary of
PRICE/STERN/SLOAN
Publishers, Inc., Los Angeles

1983

ABOUT THIS BOOK

Making homemade cartoon movies is a fun hobby. But not many of us can afford all the equipment and film needed to get started. That's why this book was created. With these simple cut-outs and a few odds and ends from around your home, you can actually construct all sorts of crazy gadgets for producing motion pictures without needing to buy anything else.

Some of the contraptions in this book are the forgotten works of mad scientists who gave them ridiculous names like "zoetrope" or "phenakistoscope". The names sound complicated, but the gadgets are simple! One device was invented by a rich man to entertain his butler's children. If you don't have a butler, you can use it to entertain your friends. Several of these movie machines are the author's own harebrained creations.

Try your hand at drawing wheels turning, people walking, smoke rising or frogs jumping. Then use your talents to put together a story told in motion. Tinker with the devices a bit. Who knows, maybe you'll invent a movie machine of your own.

MATERIALS NEEDED

Transparent tape	Spray can top	Paper
White glue	Thumbtacks	Cardboard
Pencils	Cork	Scissors
Paper clips	Spools	Hole punch
Toothpicks	Shiny plastic	Ruler

Copyright© 1975 by TROUBADOR PRESS, INC., 1 Sutter Street, San Francisco, California 91405. Distributed by PRICE/STERN/SLOAN Publishers, Inc., 410 North La Cienega Boulevard, Los Angeles, California 90048. Printed in the United States of America. All rights reserved. No part of this publication may be reproduced, stored in a retrieval system, or transmitted, in any form or by any means, electronic, mechanical, photocopying, recording, or otherwise, without the prior written permission of the publishers. ISBN: 0-8431-1710-9

The cut out pages such as this should be completely removed along the dotted line near the center fold, and the scraps can be thrown away as you complete each project. The other pages will remain bound in the book so that you'll have a complete guide book to go with your movie machines.

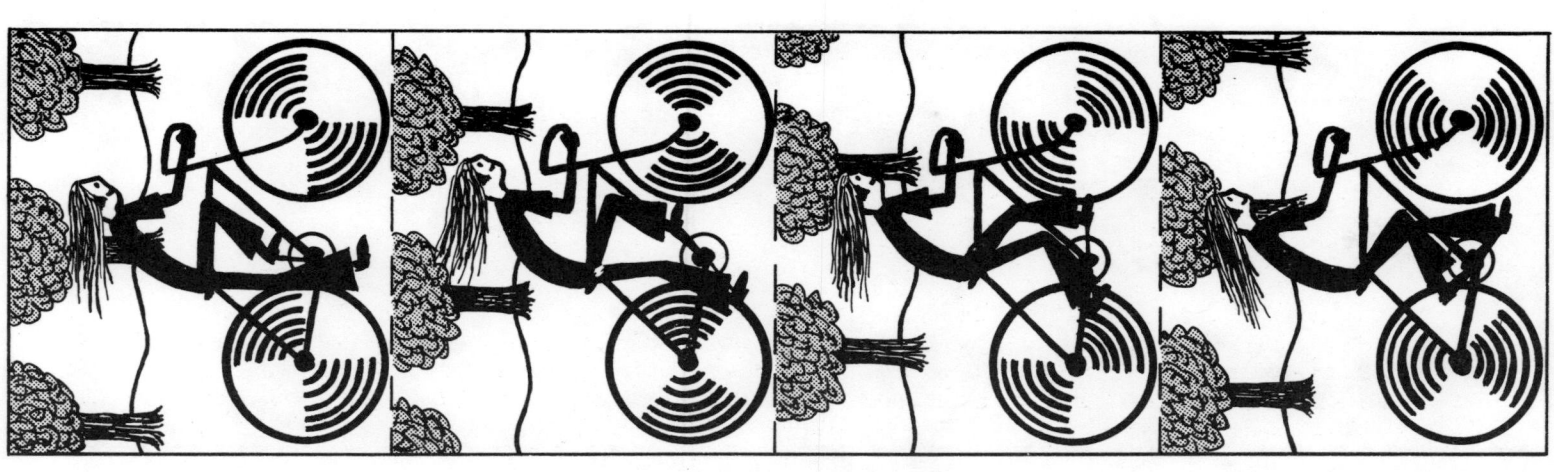

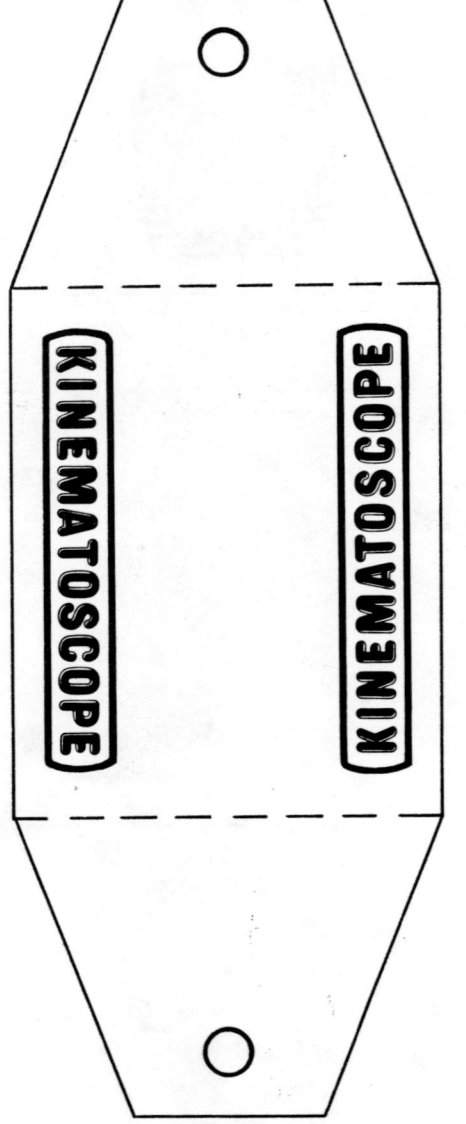

1. Cut out the piece below and tape a straightened paper clip along the stars.

2. Fold it into a paddle wheel and tape or glue it together.

3. Cut and punch the piece at the left and fold up its sides as shown to make a stand for the paddle wheel.

4. Set the paddle wheel in the stand by inserting the ends of the paper clip through the side holes. Page 5 tells how to work the **KINEMATOSCOPE**.

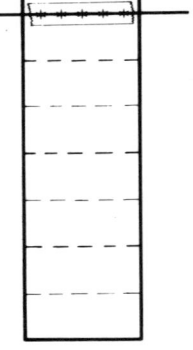
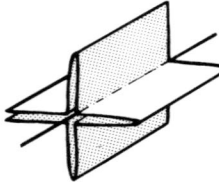
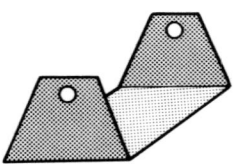

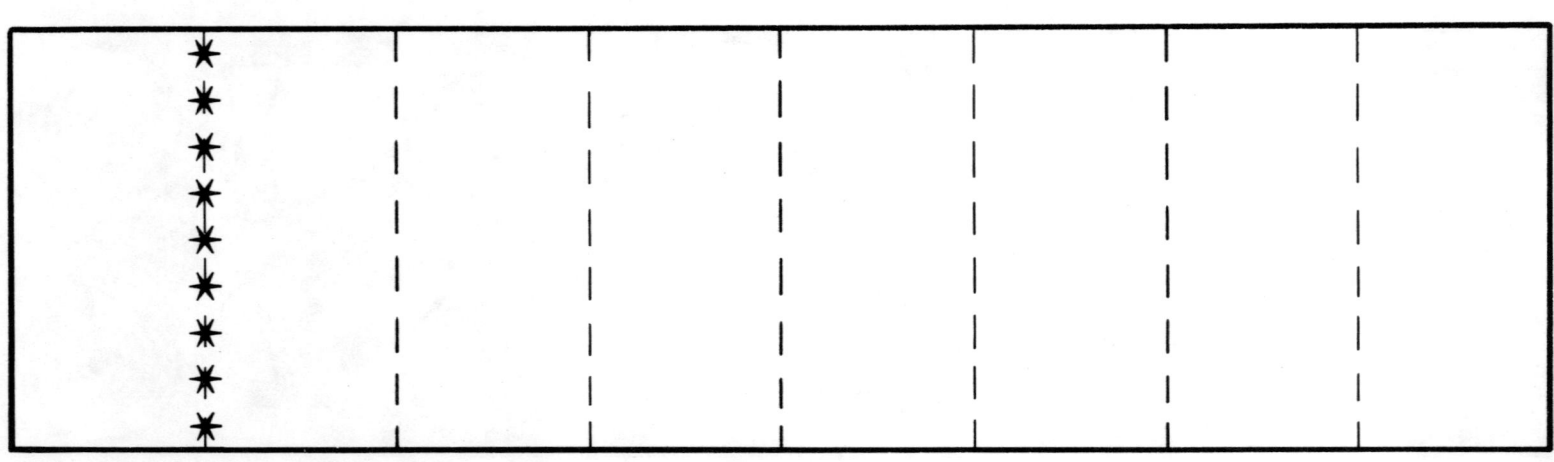

THAUMATROPE

(THAW-ma-trope)

The THAUMATROPE is an old toy that doesn't show motion, but it will help you understand how motion pictures work.

Cut out the discs on page 4 and attach strings where the dots are. When you twirl a disc by the strings, you will see both sides at once. Why? This is because of *persistence of vision.* One picture stays in your eyes for a short time after the other picture flips into view. The eyes are fooled into thinking they see both pictures at the same time.

Operating a THAUMATROPE. (Private collection of Dr. Martin Perl)

Five people claimed to be the inventor of this toy, starting around 1826. Several of them got the idea by noticing that a spinning coin shows both faces at the same time. Try it. It works best if you hold your eyes down at the level of the table top where the coin is spinning.

A completed KINEMATOSCOPE.

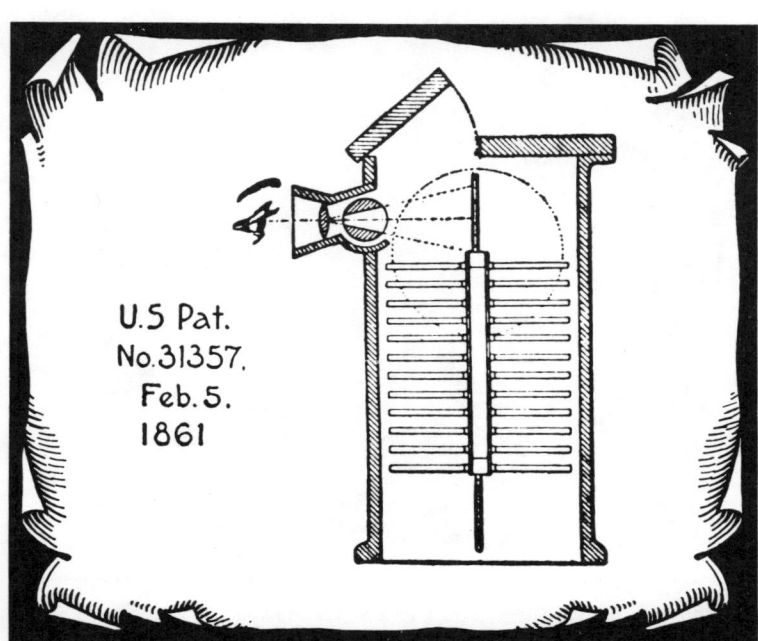

KINEMATOSCOPE

(Kin-a-MAT-o-scope)

The KINEMATOSCOPE works just like the gadget above, but it gives the illusion of motion because it has four pictures showing things in changed positions.

Follow the directions on page 4. Then set the stand so the paddle wheel is facing you, and gently rotate the paper clip. You will see the rider's legs move and the wheels turn. The pictures change so rapidly that your eyes are fooled. Try it in different lighting and at different speeds to get the best effect.

The drawing at the lower left shows how an inventor attached more pictures to this device to smooth out the motion and lengthen the movie.

PHENAKISTOSCOPE
(Fen-a-KIST-o-scope)

The next two gadgets are different versions of the same toy. They're called **PHENAKISTOSCOPES**. Follow the directions for making them on pages 7 and 9.

To work the first one, hold it by the handle and spin it while looking through the slits toward a mirror. The cartoon pictures that you see in the mirror will spring to life.

The second gadget you hold by the center spool, and then spin the pencil with your free hand while looking through the slits toward the other disc.

You can also use the cut-outs as patterns for making movie discs of your own. Page 11 gives you some suggestions for drawing the motion pictures.

The **PHENAKISTOSCOPE** which dates back to 1832 is probably the oldest device to actually produce motion pictures. Oddly enough, the inventor, Joseph Plateau, was partially blind. Earlier in life he had stared at the sun for 20 minutes to test out his persistence of vision. The sun's glaring image stayed in his eyes for several weeks after that, not because of persistence of vision, but because the bright rays had burned holes in the backs of his eyes! In the months that followed, his eyesight grew progressively worse, and it was during this period that he dreamed up his ingenious way of producing motion pictures.

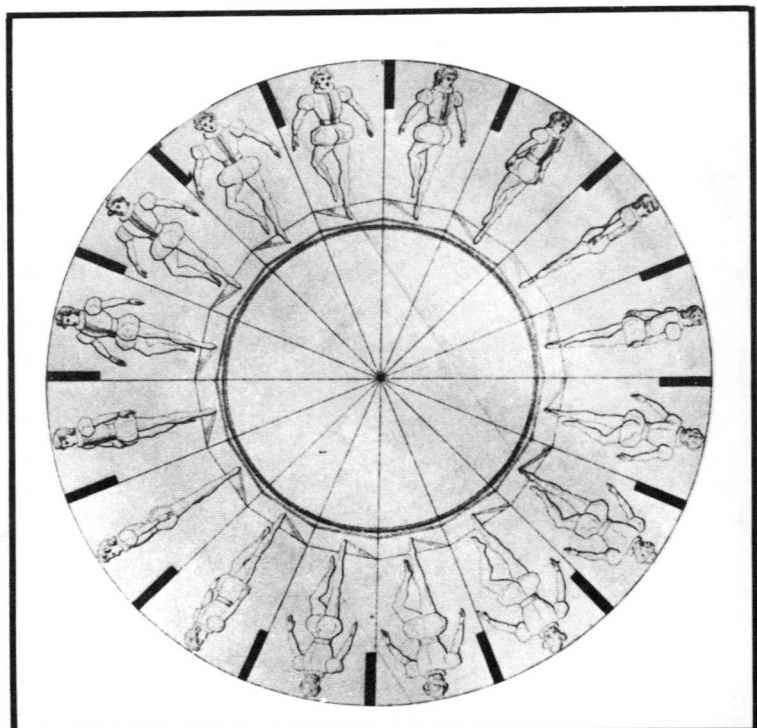

Plateau's first PHENAKISTOSCOPE.

1. Cut out the disc, and make slits where the marks are like this: []

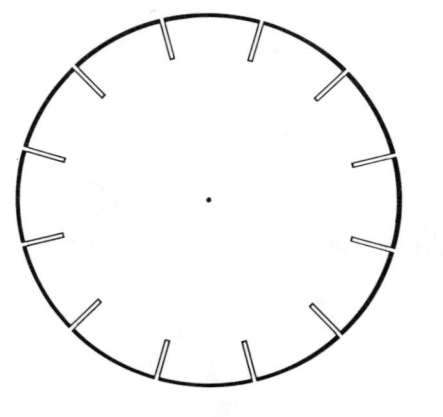

2. Make a handle by thumbtacking to a pencil eraser like this. Page 6 tells how to work this **PHENAKISTO-SCOPE**.

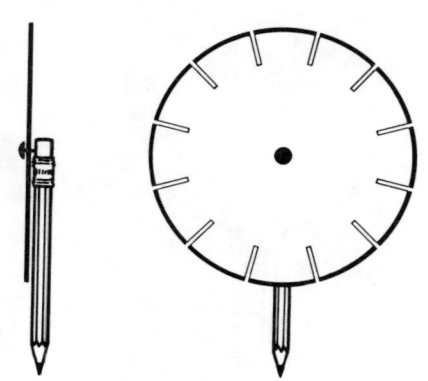

Add color for best results.

Here are some other ways to make a handle from a stick of wood, a spool or a worn-out pencil eraser.

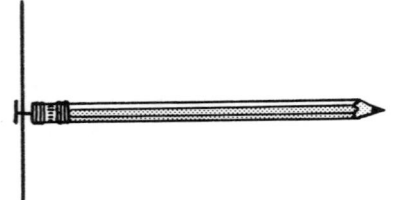

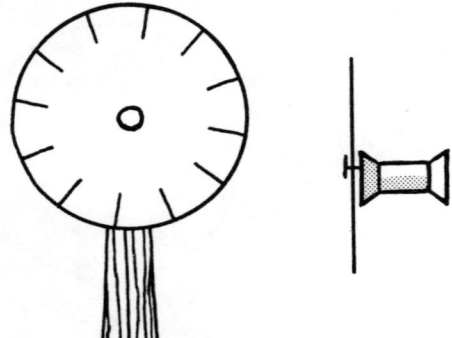

If you make more of these movie discs, be sure to color one side black like the one below.

THE AMAZING PHENAKISTOSCOPE

1. Cut out both discs and make slits where the marks are like this: ▯

   Then glue a spool to each disc.

   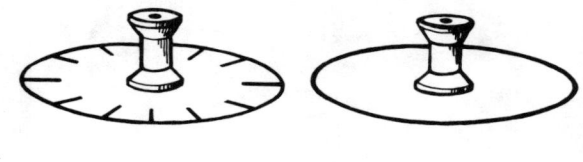

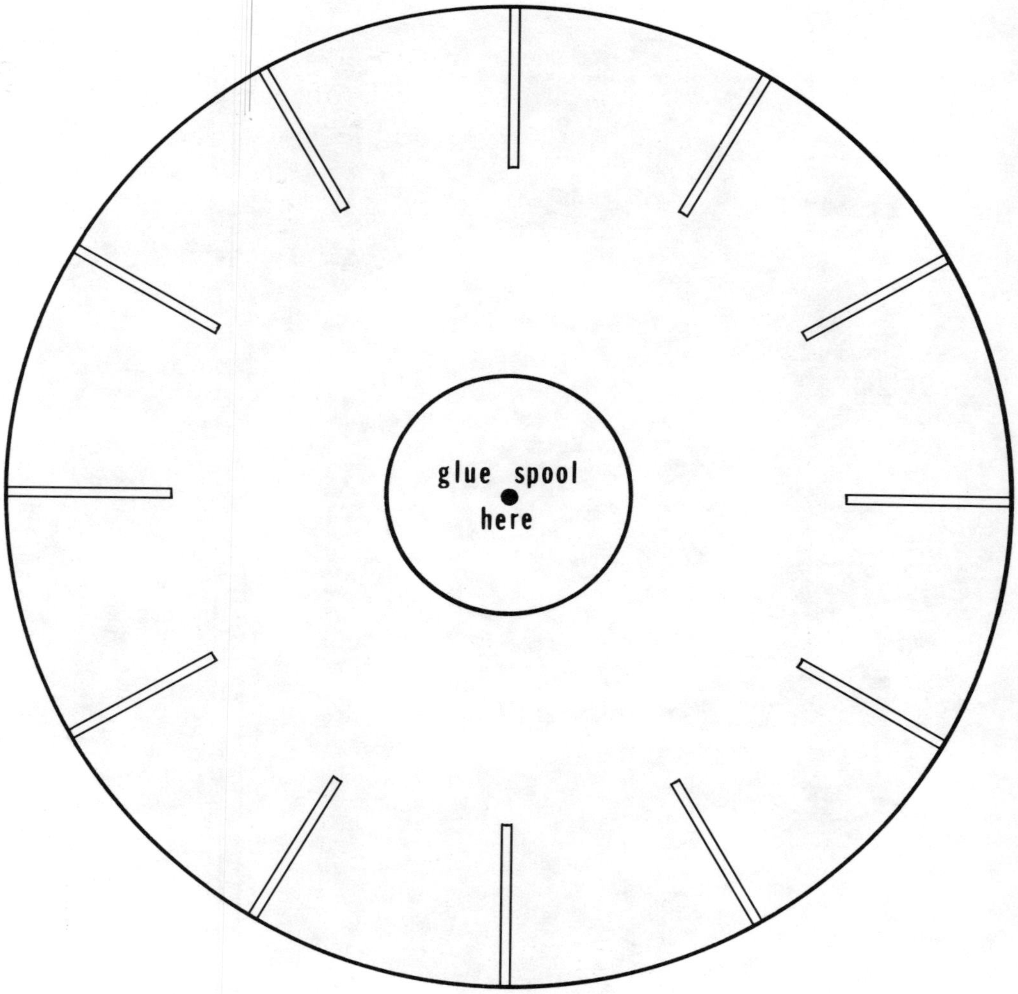

2. Slide a loosely fitting spool onto a pencil, and fit the discs you just made onto the pencil's ends. The ends can be tightened by wrapping a little tape around them. Page 6 tells how to work this **PHENAKIS-TOSCOPE**.

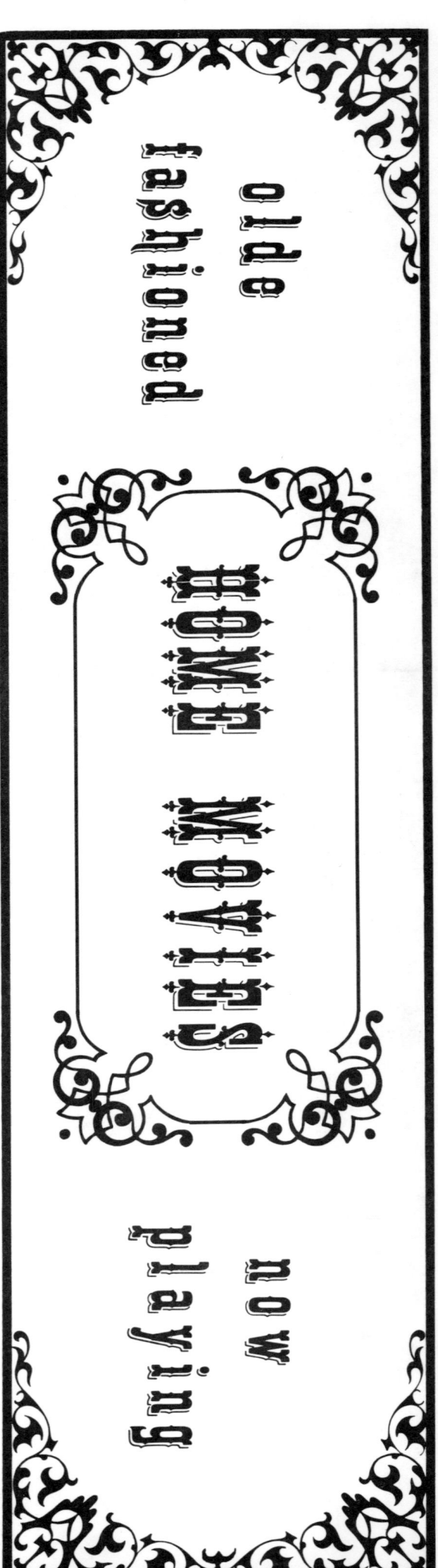

Lobby card or banner to cut out.

SUGGESTIONS FOR DRAWING YOUR OWN MOVIE CARTOONS

START SIMPLE!

Here's a good one to try — a balloon getting larger and larger and then popping.

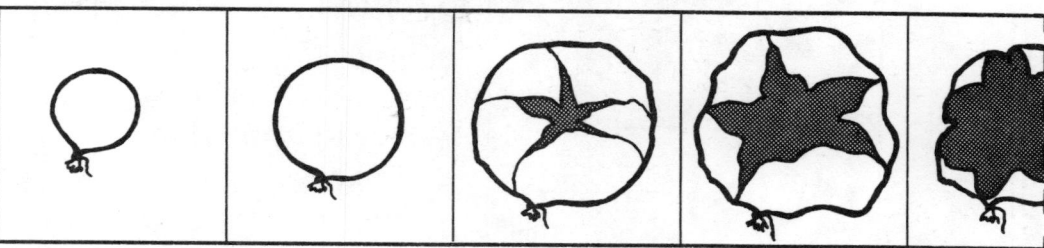

Smoke rising is another subject with which to start.

Try this — draw the side view of a person. Then show his arm moving up and down bouncing a ball.

When you draw a fish swimming, move it forward a little bit in each picture so that it appears to glide through the water.

A wheel turning is easy to draw. Move it forward in each picture as you did with the fish.

The wheel you just finished drawing now becomes a unicycle with a rider.

Drawing people walking or running takes a little practice, but even your first attempt will be loads of fun to view.

11

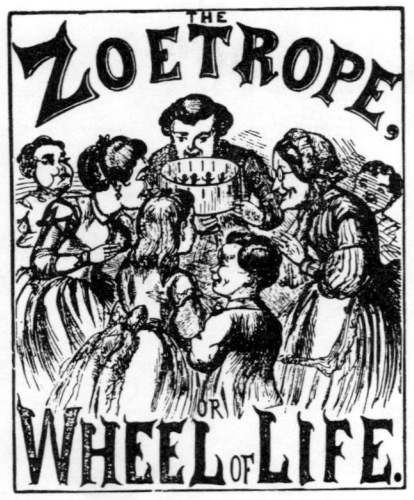

The next page shows you how to make a **ZOETROPE**. Spin it and look through the slits to make the horses gallop along the race track. This eye-dazzling machine was invented twice — first by William Horner in England around 1834, where people called it the "wheel of the devil", and again by Pierre Desvignes in 1860 France, where it was renamed the **ZOETROPE** meaning "wheel of life".

The galloping horse movie shown in your **ZOETROPE** was "filmed" back in 1878, long before movie cameras had been invented. The photographer, Edweard Muybridge, lined up a whole row of cameras along a race track and connected strings across the track to operate the shutter mechanisms. When he sent a horse galloping past the cameras, it hit the strings and "clicked" the cameras in rapid sequence to produce the series of pictures used here. Muybridge found that a **ZOETROPE** is just the right tool for showing his horse movies.

The whole experiment is said to have started because Governor Leland Stanford of California bet somebody $25,000 that a horse has all four of its feet off the ground during part of its gallop. He hired Muybridge to prove it and won the bet. Look at the horse photos and you will see that he was right.

An original 19th century ZOETROPE. (Private collection of American Zoetrope Film Facility)

Setting up for the galloping horse movie. (Courtesy of Stanford University)

1. Cut out the two straight pieces and make slits where the marks are like this: ▯   Tape them together to make a cylinder.

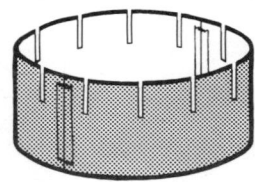

2. Cut out the disc and strengthen it by gluing to another disc of stiff cardboard. Then tape the disc securely to the bottom of the cylinder.

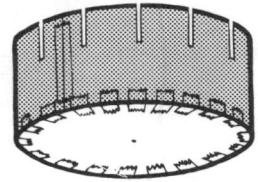

3. Attach the cylinder to a plastic spray can top using a thumbtack. Never push a thumbtack into a spray can itself.

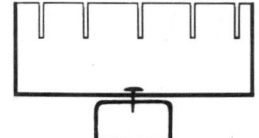

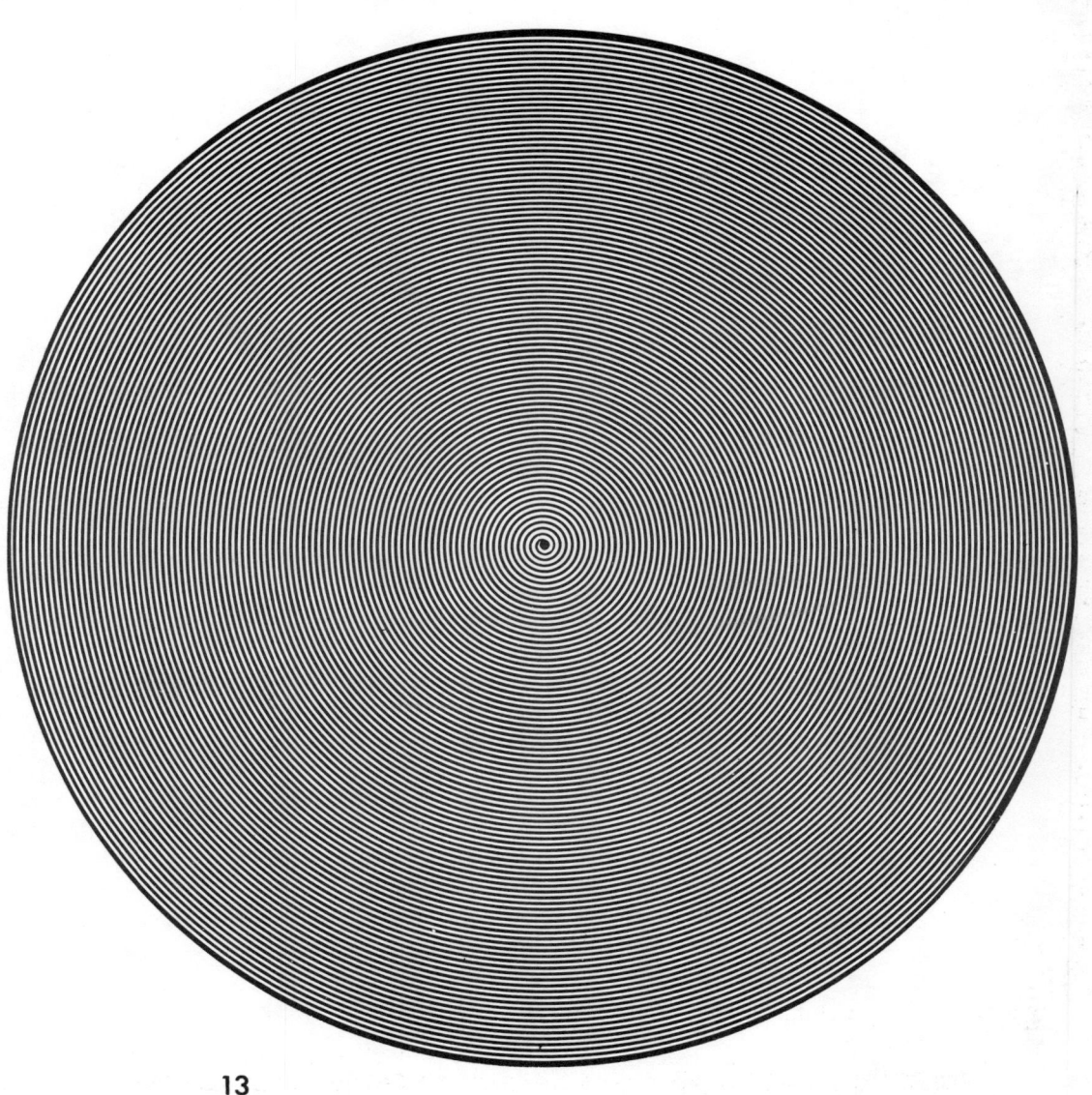

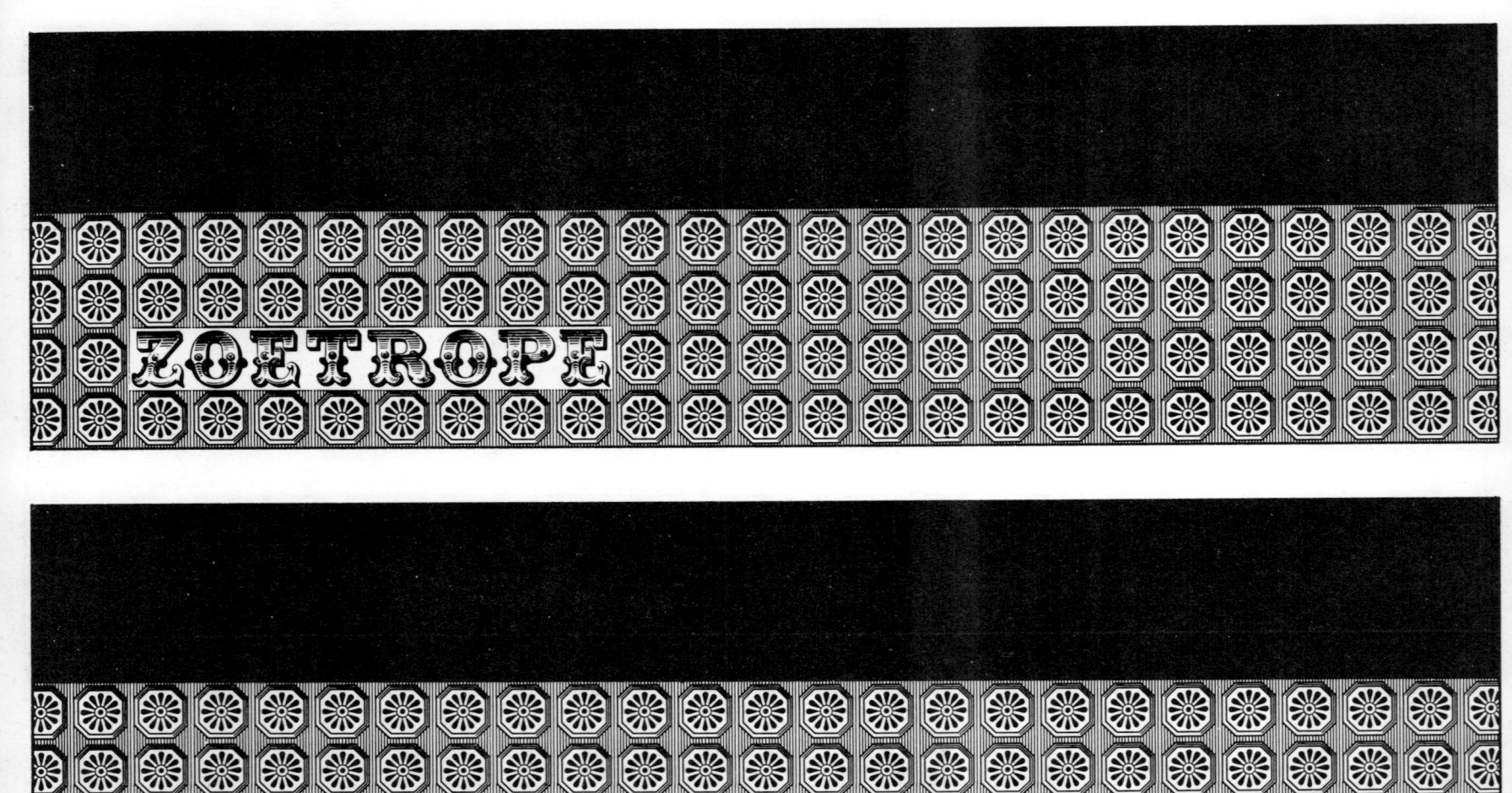

Page 15 gives you extra movie strips to use with your ZOE-TROPE. Cut them out and tape each pair into a single strip.

The strip will fit along the inside of the ZOETROPE where the horse photos are now. You can also make your own movie strips from pieces of paper 18 inches long. Draw the pictures evenly spaced 1½ inches wide.

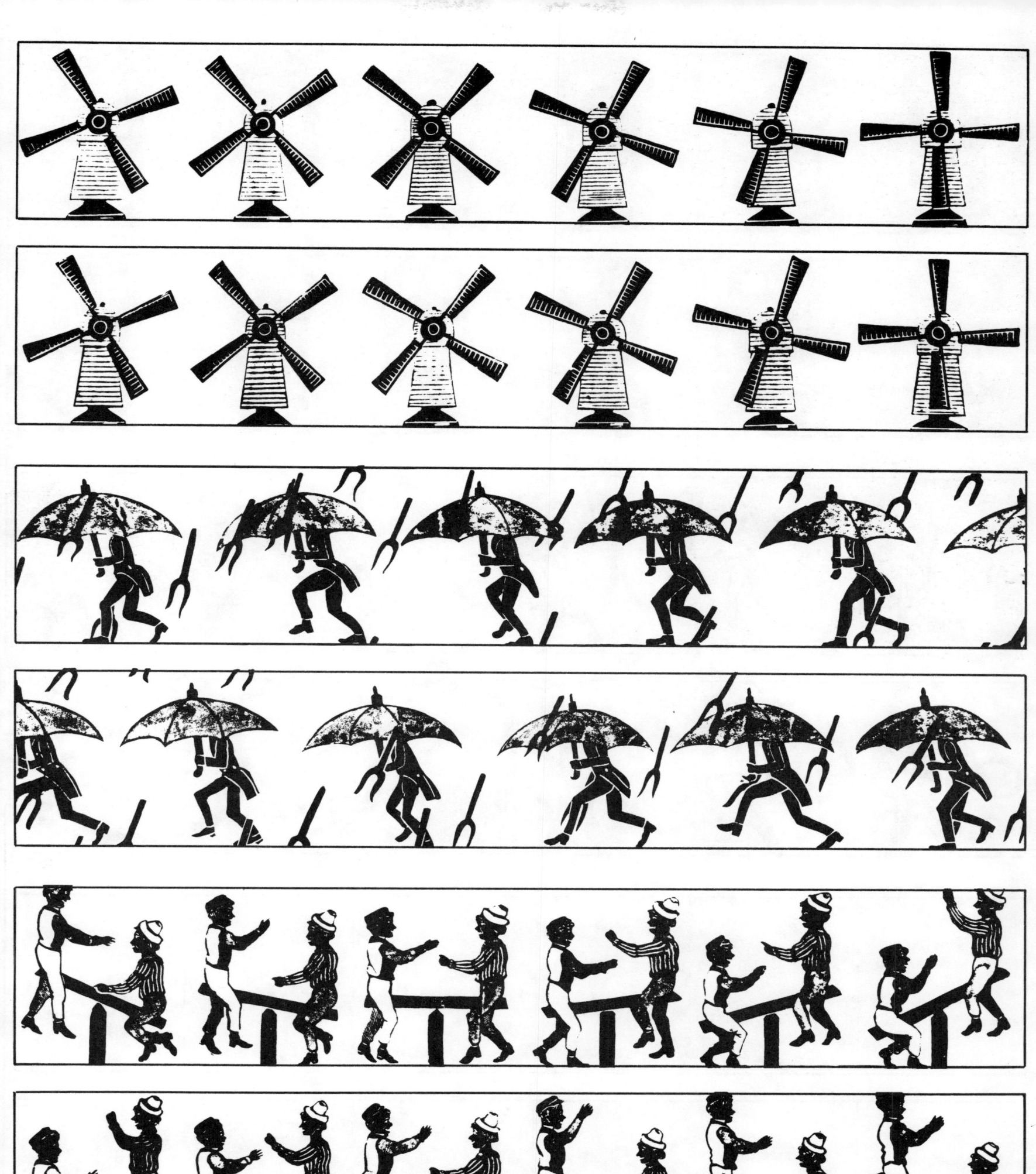

19th century ZOETROPE strips. (Courtesy of The Oakland Museum)

Use this strip to draw your own movie cartoon.

A FLIP-IT

1. Find some paper thinner than this page and cut two pieces the size of the drawings below. Trace the woodpecker and tree onto those pieces with a felt pen or dark crayon.

2. Roll one piece around a pencil until it is completely rolled up.

To work your **FLIP-IT**, place the curled picture on top of the flat picture and rapidly slide a pencil back and forth as shown. As the top piece flips up and down, your eyes see the woodpecker "peck" the tree.

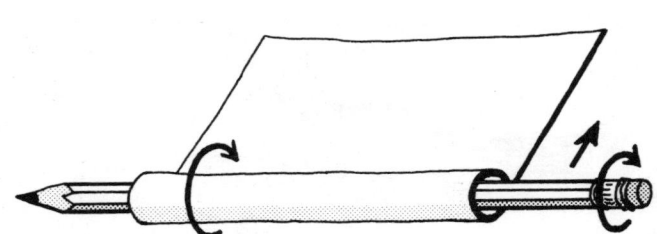
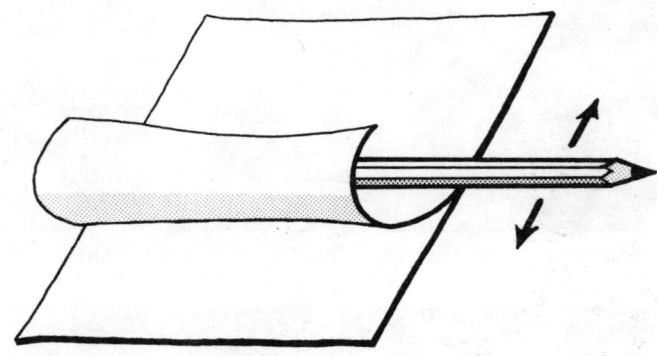

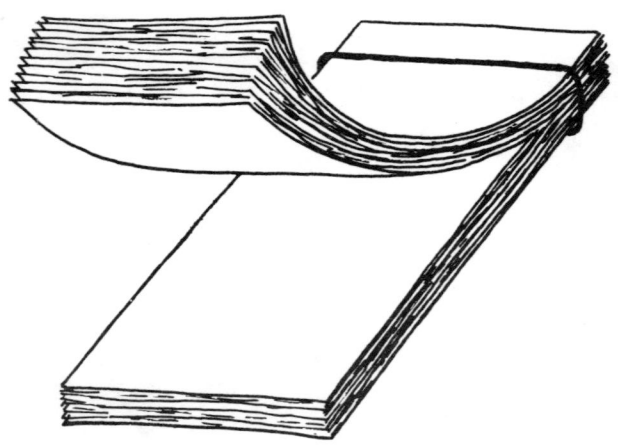

KINEOGRAPH
(KIN-e-o-graph)

(Courtesy of Musee Mecanique, San Francisco)

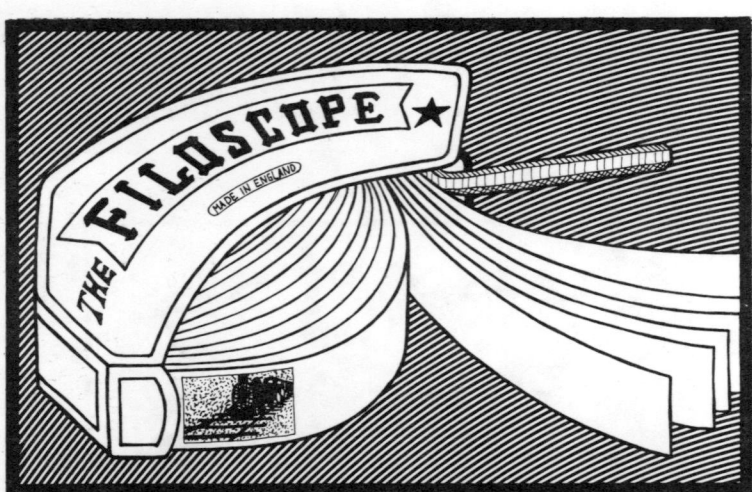

The **KINEOGRAPH** is more commonly known as the "flip-book". You can make this movie machine by carefully cutting apart all the pieces on pages 19 and 21 and stacking them up like a deck of cards. Tap the end of the deck on a table to even up the pieces, and fasten them together with a rubber band. Then just flip through the stack with your thumb to watch the action!

The "flip-book" was first patented in 1868 but may have been in use a long time before that. Fancier versions of this simple toy became a popular entertainment around the turn of the century. Peep-show movie parlors lined with rows of coin operated **MUTOSCOPES** like the one shown upper left sprang up across the United States and Europe. Put a nickel in the slot and you could watch a thrilling train robbery or a comedy act. For home use there was the **FILOSCOPE** shown center left, and the **KINORA** shown lower left.

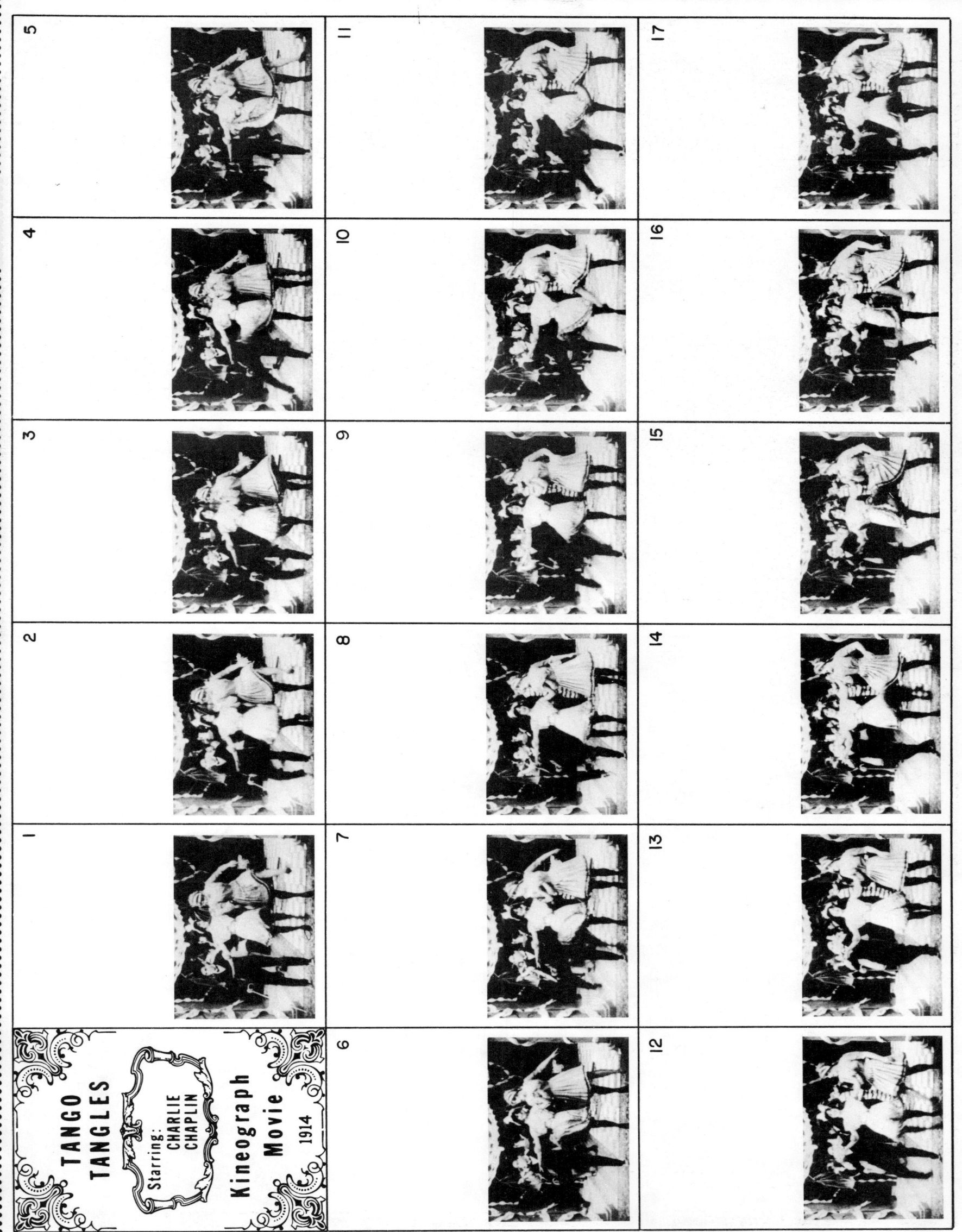

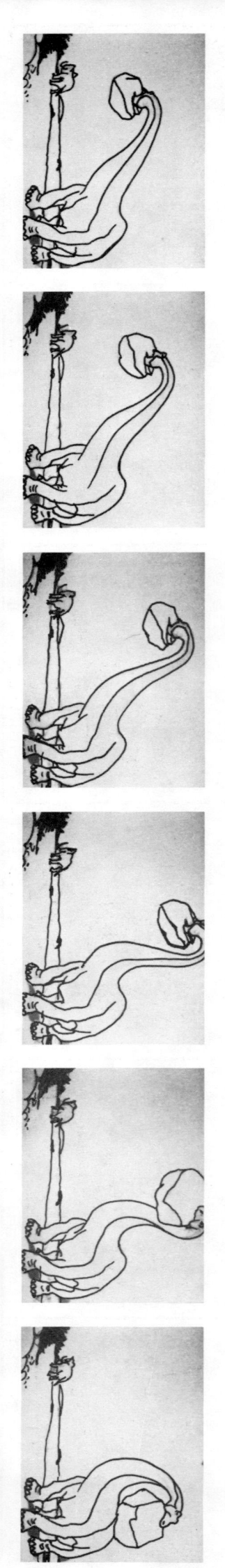
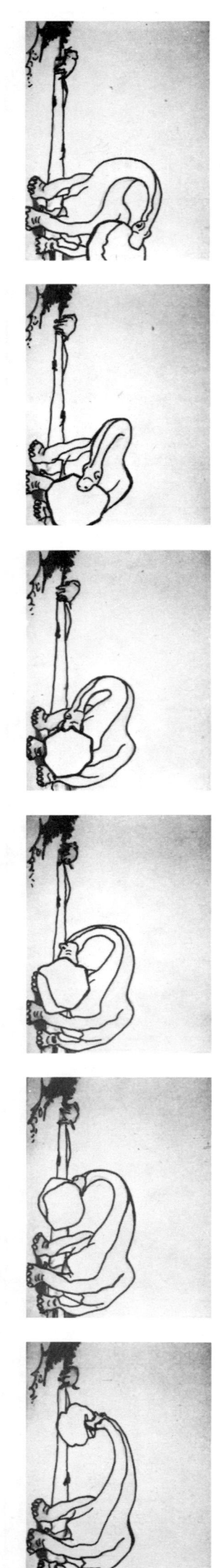
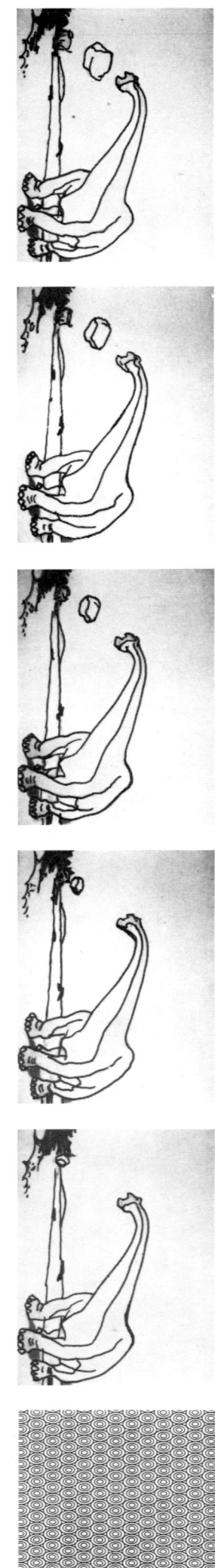

20

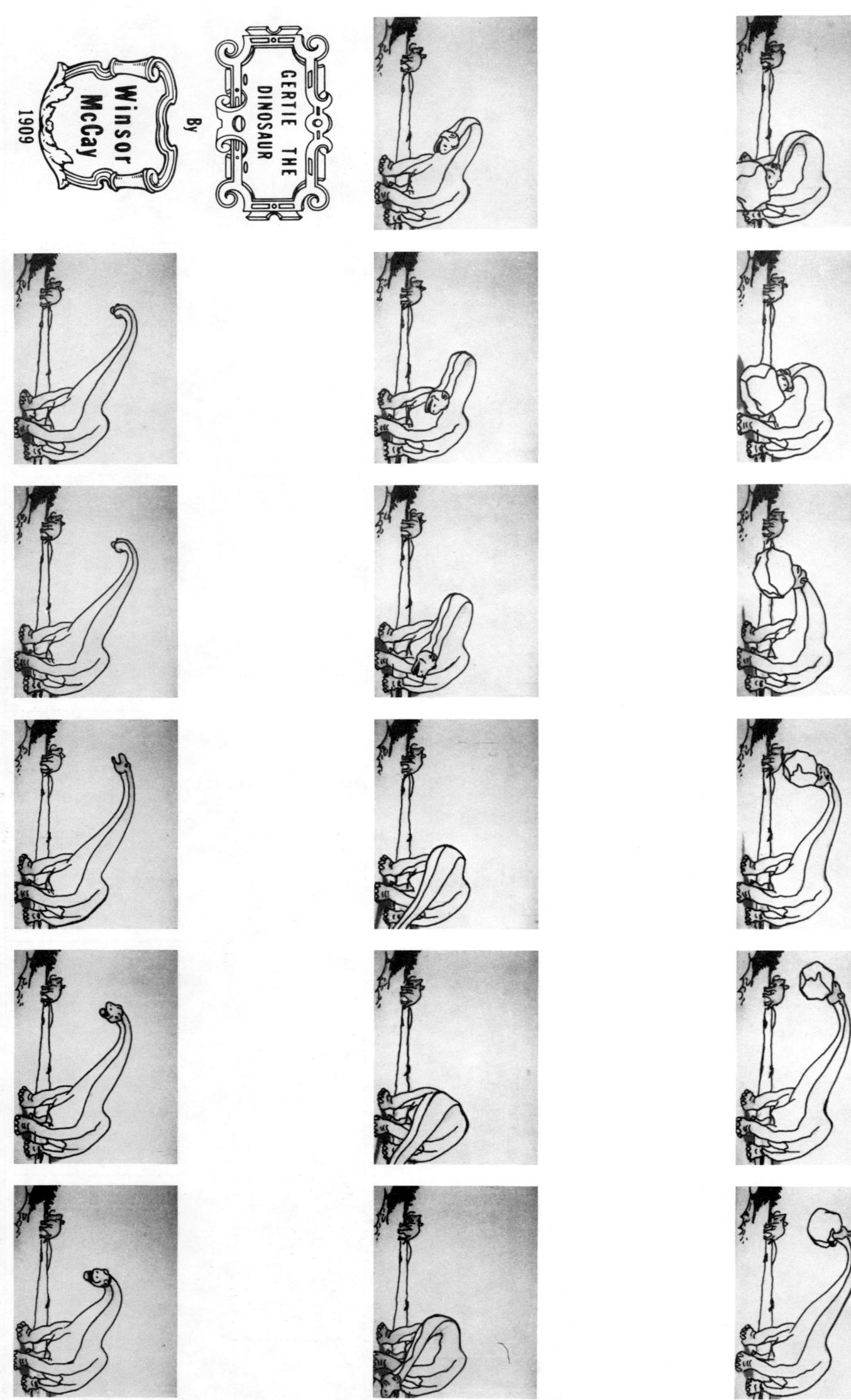

ROLLOSCOPE
(ROLL-o-scope)

1. Cut out the three strips, and fold them back and forth along the broken lines to make flexible joints. Tape them together with the pieces *not quite* touching like this.

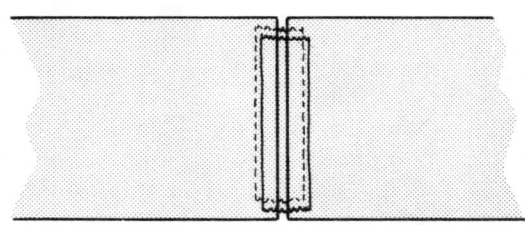

2. Tape a straightened paper clip along the stars, and tape a nickel, or other equal weight, to the other end.

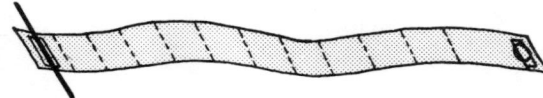

To view the movie, roll up the strip, and hold it in front of you with the free end hanging down in back. Now let the strip unroll, and the action begins!

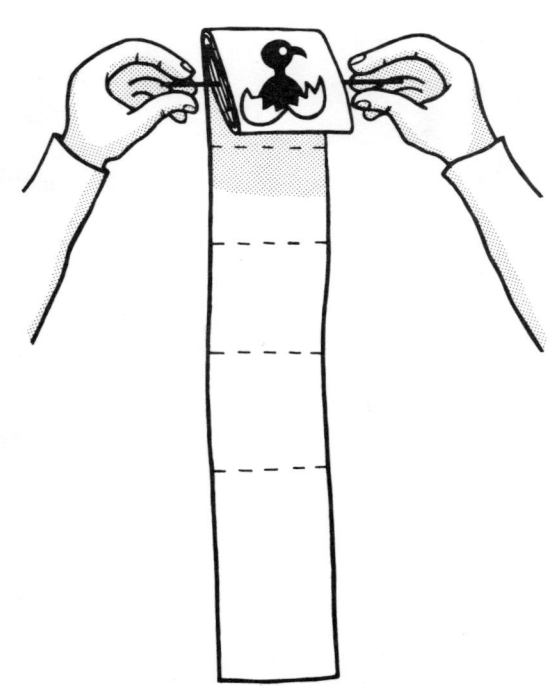

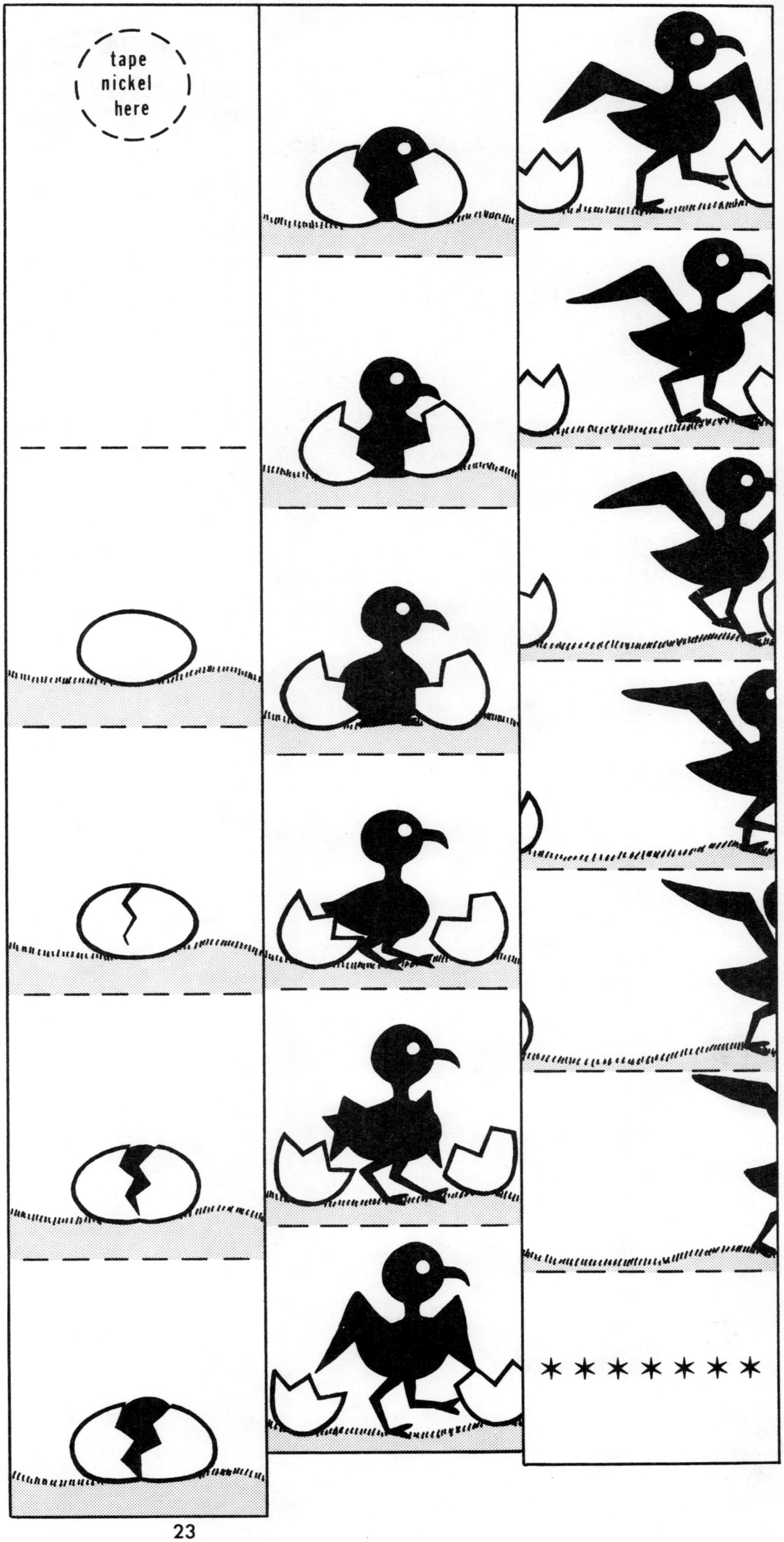

Instructions on page 27.

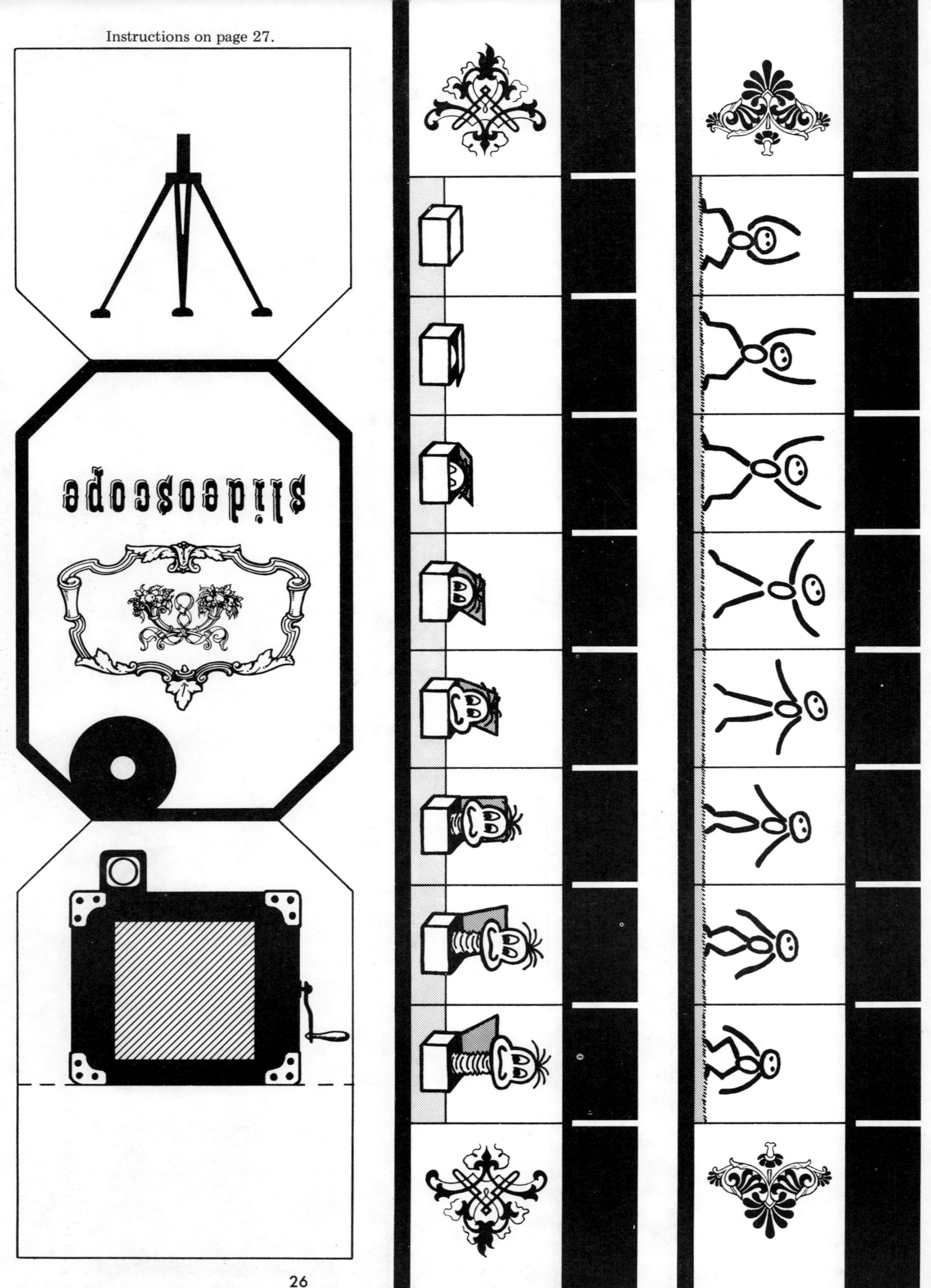

SLIDEOSCOPE

(SLIDE-o-scope)

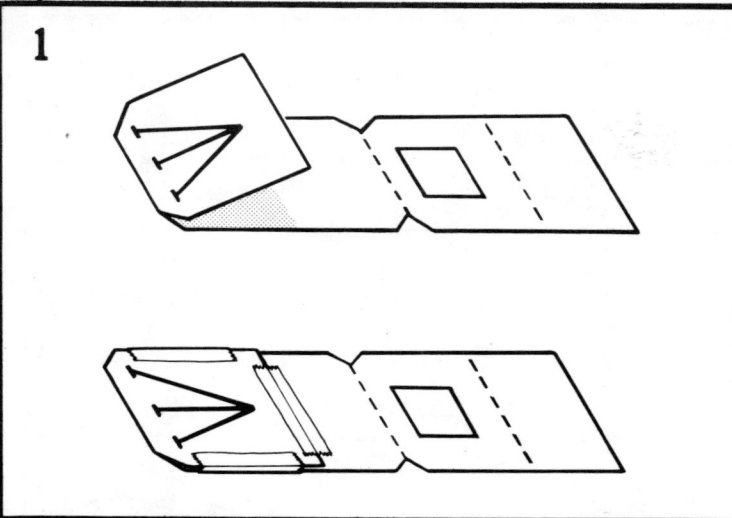

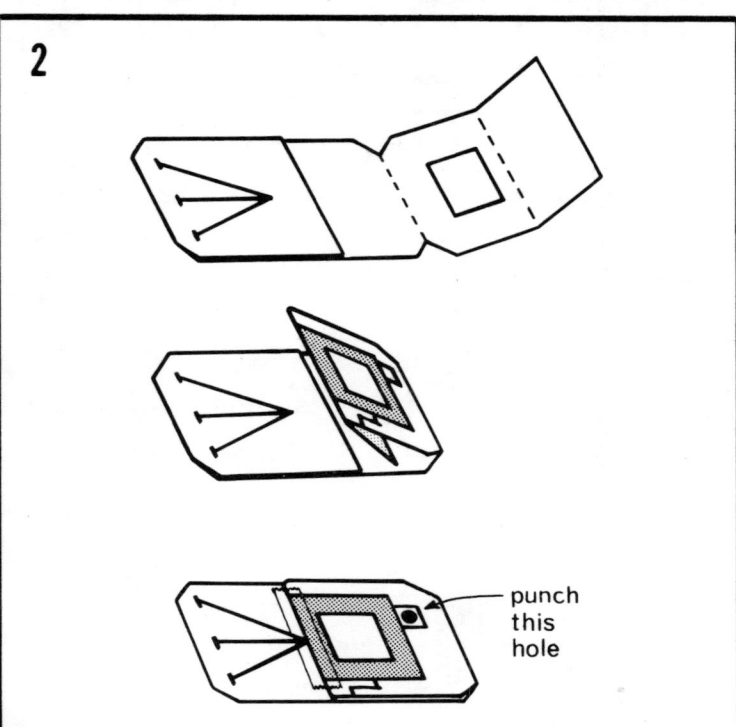

punch this hole

1. Cut out the piece at the outer edge of page 26 and remove the square that looks like this: ▨ Do not punch the holes yet. Fold and tape as shown in drawing 1.

2. Then fold and tape once more as shown in drawing 2. Now punch out both holes with a hole punch.

3. Cut out the film strips and make slits where the marks are like this:

To view your movies, look through the peep-hole toward a well lit mirror, and slide a filmstrip back and forth in the holder. Slide strip at different speeds for best effect.

You may want to reinforce these filmstrips by gluing strips of cardboard along the back sides.

PRAXINOSCOPE
(Prak-SIN-o-scope)

The **PRAXINOSCOPE** movie machine is a remarkable device that works with tiny rotating mirrors. You can get these mirrors from a piece of shiny plastic. Aluminized plastic from an art store is best, but a piece of shiny black plastic or a stiff see-through box top painted black on one side with a felt marker will work too. Aluminum foil is a little too flimsy to work effectively.

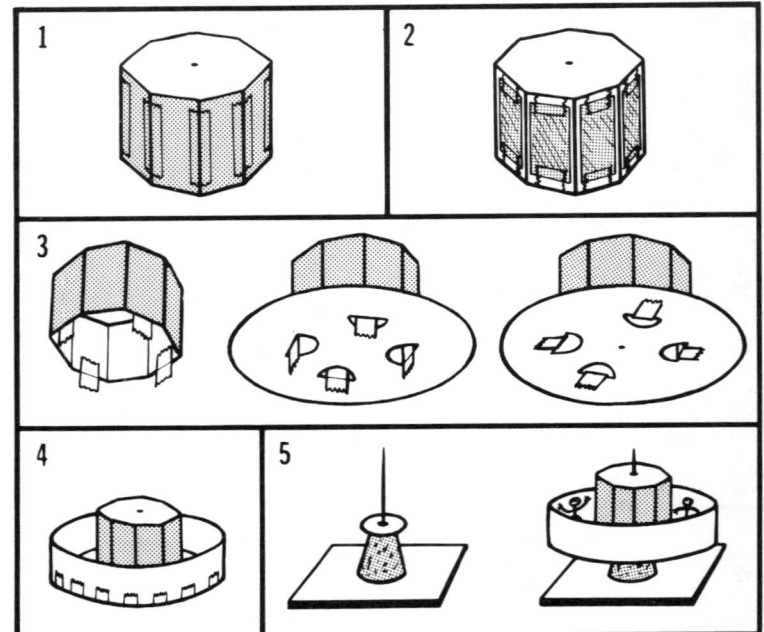

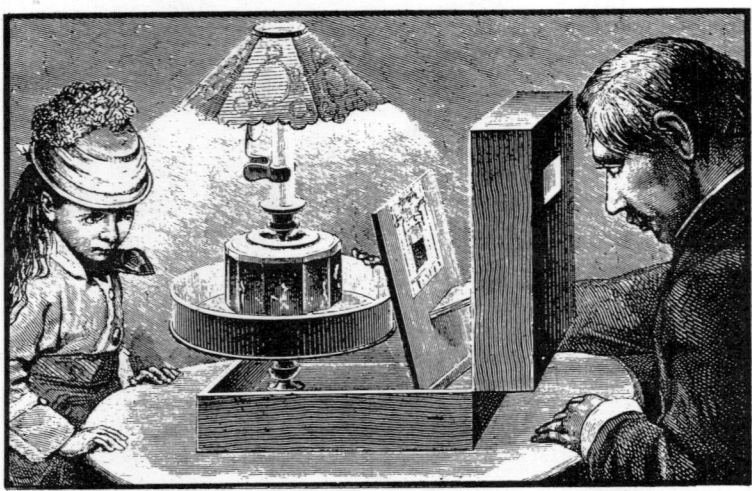
Toy PRAXINOSCOPE theater. (Private collection of Dr. Martin Perl)

Reynaud's PRAXINOSCOPE movie house named "Theatre Optique".

In 1892, inventor Emile Reynaud used his **PRAXINOSCOPE** to open the world's first movie theater in Paris. He combined the invention with a magic lantern for projecting movies which he drew on long strips of special translucent paper.

1. Cut out the 8 sided piece on page 29 and punch the center with a toothpick. Then fold and tape to look like drawing 1.

2. Cut 8 mirrors the size shown by the pattern. Fasten them to the 8 sided piece with tape just like you see in drawing 2, making sure they lie flat.

3. Cut out the larger disc; punch the center with a toothpick; and tape it to the 8 sided piece as shown in 3.

4. Cut out the strip that looks like this:

and tape it along the edge of the disc to form a rim as shown in 4. Then cut out the cartoon strips and insert one of them along the inside of the rim.

5. Make a stand by gluing a cork to a piece of stiff cardboard and then pushing a toothpick into the cork as shown in 5. Slip the small disc and then the **PRAXINOSCOPE** onto the toothpick.

Now just spin the **PRAXINOSCOPE** and watch the cartoon movie reflected in the mirrors. It works best under a bright light. You may have to reposition the cartoon strip to center the pictures at the right spot on the mirrors.

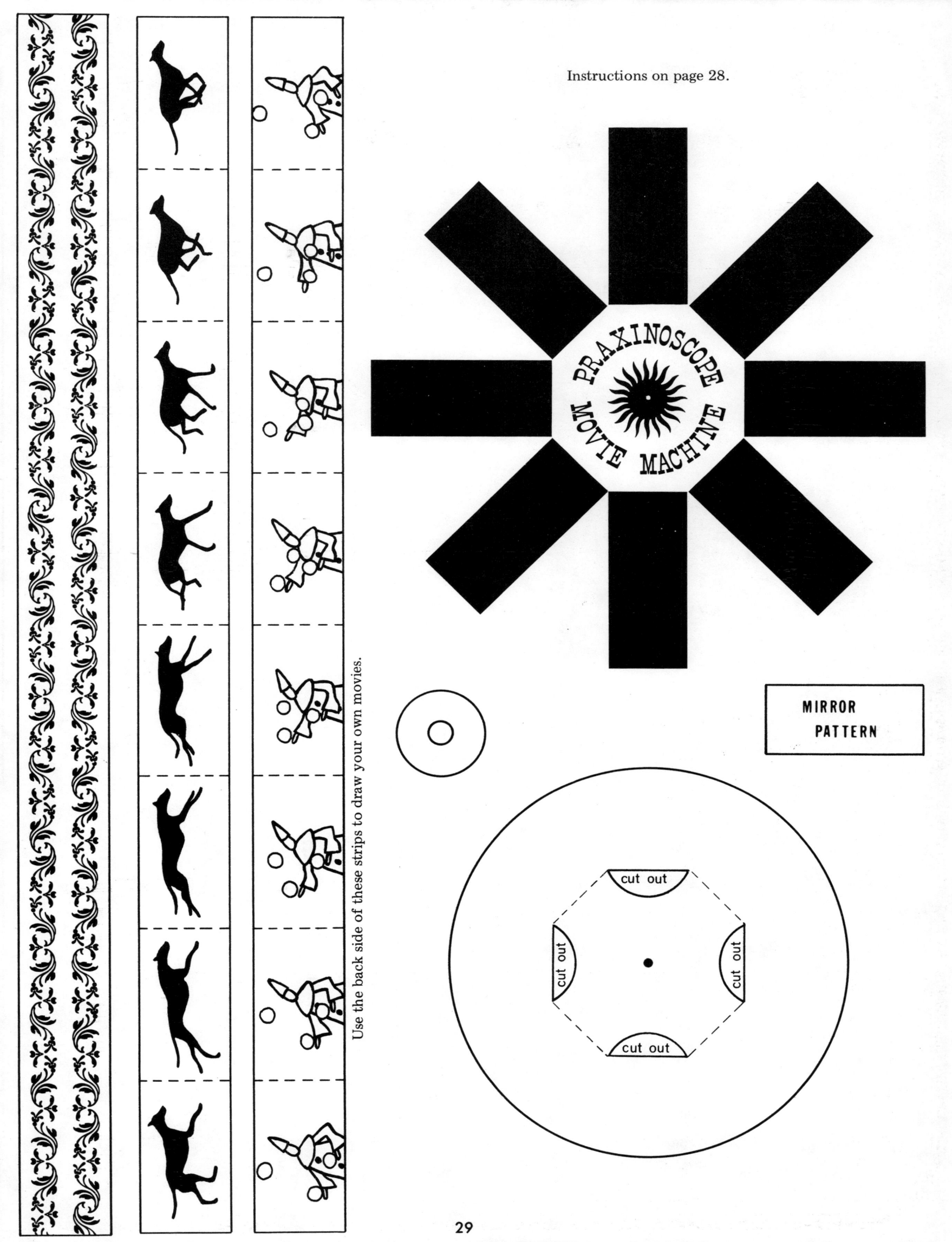

ADDING LENGTH TO YOUR MOVIES

After you have experimented with the cut-out devices in this book and mastered the basics of animation, you may want to try your hand at drawing longer movies. The simplest way to lengthen your movies is by making extra thick flip-books. 3 x 5 index cards are perfect for this. With a stack of 200 cards, your movie will run for about 10 to 20 seconds. Longer movies can be continued on the other side and then to additional stacks of cards.

Keep in mind that for each *second* of running time you will need to draw about 15 pictures. Movies shown in theaters require even more — 24 each second, which adds up to 130,000 pictures for a 90 minute movie! This is not meant to discourage you, but only to help you direct your talents toward realistic goals. Some of the most creative animated films have been stories lasting under a minute.

Before you draw your movie, it's a good idea to first sketch out a storyboard in comic strip fashion to help develop the characters and coordinate the action. The storyboard below is an example of what one might look like for a 15 second movie. Notice that it is only used to show *general plot* — not each and every movement of the whole film.

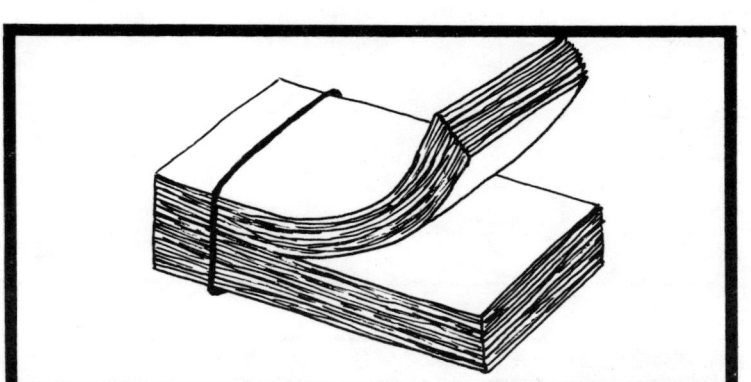

ADVANCED PROJECT

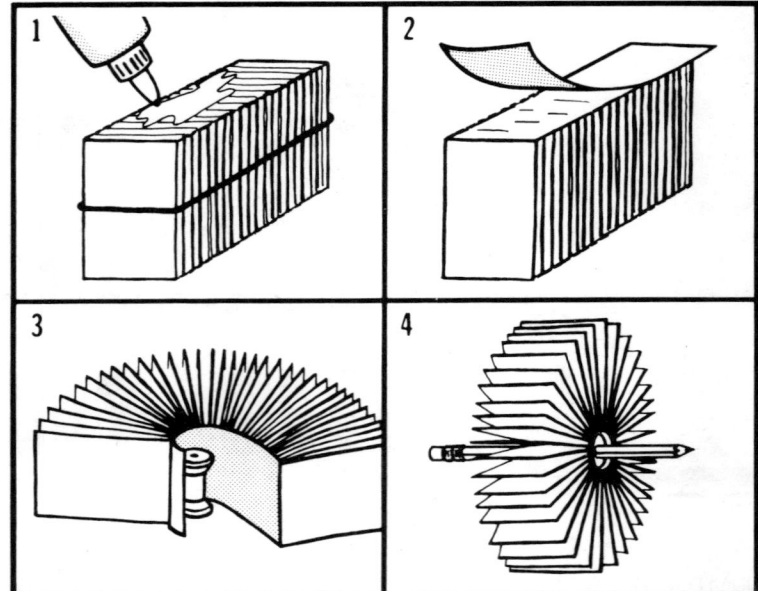

Here's how to make a **KINORA** for showing a movie lasting about 60 seconds. You will need a stack of index cards 3 to 4 inches thick. Rubberband the cards together; even up the ends by tapping them on a table; and then smear lots of white glue over the upper edge of the stack as shown in drawing 1. After the glue is dry, apply still more and fasten down a card strip to form a binding as shown in 2. Let one end of the binding card extend beyond the end of the stack. When everything is completely dry, wrap the cards around a spool and cut off just enough cards to make a tight fit. Then glue the binding to the spool and allow to dry. Insert a tight fitting pencil through the spool.

Find a box or construct one to hold the spool and cards as shown. Notice the opening for viewing the movie and the small flap that holds the cards down just before they flip up. After you have drawn a series of cartoon pictures on the cards, you can view the movie by very slowly rotating the pencil in the direction of the arrow.

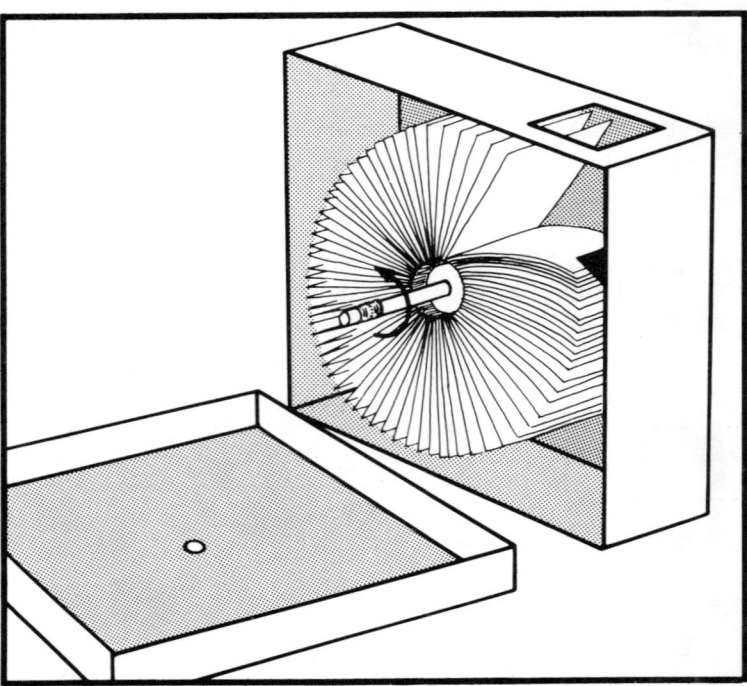

Troubador Press books are available from book, gift, toy, art material, museum and department stores, or may be ordered directly by sending check or money order for the total amount plus $1.00 for handling and mailing. For a complete list of titles send a *stamped self-addressed envelope* to:

 **TROUBADOR PRESS, INC., SAN FRANCISCO**
in care of
PRICE/STERN/SLOAN *Publishers, Inc.*
410 North La Cienega Boulevard, Los Angeles, California 90048
DIRECT MAIL DEPT.

32